Folded Book Art
made easy

Recycling books into beautiful folded sculptures

Marta Decker

© 2018

by

Marta Decker

All rights reserved. No portion of this book may be reproduced, stored in a retrieval system, or transmitted in any form or by any means--electronic, mechanical, photocopy, recording, scanning, or other--except for brief quotations in critical reviews or articles, without the prior written permission of the publisher.

ISBN 978-0-578-43524-4

Layout design by Dawn Boone @ boonecreative.com

Permissions obtained for the following images:

Image on pages 8-9 and center/cover by Anna Moos,

image of book with "Magical" on page 34

by Jo Ellen Schaeffer, "book in dirt" on page 17 by Linnaea Mallette

Free grunge background from Vecteezy.com

Rabbit artwork on wall on page 44 by Dawn Boone

Background setting for images on pages 107 & 115 courtesy Pomegranate Home & Garden, Bend, OR

Contents

Foreword 1

Developing Ideas 5

Picking the Right Book 13

Finding a Pattern 27

How to Fold a Book 39

Practice Session 61

Just for Fun 81

Tips and Tricks 89

Patterns 95

Resources 135

Foreword

If you grabbed this book off the shelf, I'm guessing it's because you're the kind of person who enjoys giving personal gifts and putting yourself into your gifts. You've seen folded book art, puzzled over how it's done, and wondered if this is perhaps out of your league. It looks too hard and too time-consuming. So you give up on the idea.

Then you think of your best friend who has everything money can buy and figure it's worth a try to hand them something unique—made by you. Or you consider turning that trashy series you regret reading into something valuable. You muster up the patience and decide to give it a try.

I have good news for you. While book folding looks complicated, I've developed a simplified method with some tricks and shortcuts to make book folding so much easier.

This book is a result of years of developing and fine-turning my book folding method and of teaching others to develop their skills more quickly. The feedback received from students helped me design the lessons in this book.

I am confident that book-folding *is* for you. The instructions in this book will show you just how simple it can be.

Marta

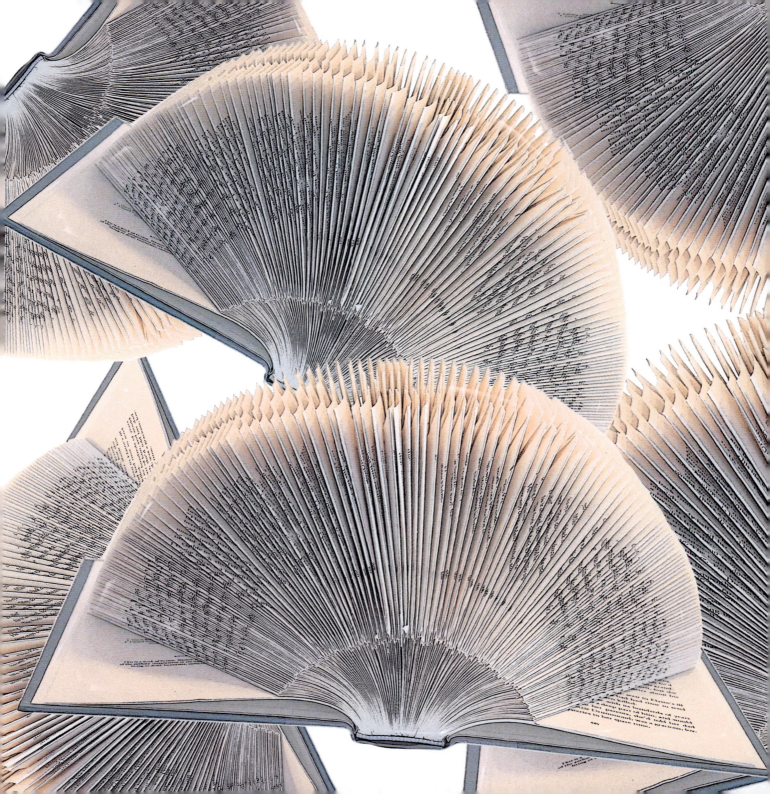

Ideas *for* Folded Books

DEVELOPING IDEAS

Developing Ideas

There are numerous occasions for giving or displaying folded books. Whether you are personalizing a gift, commemorating a special date, or creating a unique decoration for your home, there are almost infinite creative options for making a folded book that fits the occasion.

I often get requests for patterns with significant dates or someone's initials or even a team logo. I've even transformed someone's wispy signature into a book pattern, then folded it into a book on the person's favorite topic.

Every once in a while, the content of the book itself is part of the point of the gift, and then you get to double the value of the book by folding it into a second message.

Don't worry about the lack of ideas. Once you get the knack of book folding, ideas will come at you faster than your fingers can fold them.

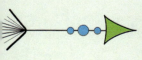 Books can be personalized with initials, words, or dates—or books can be purely decorative, like this birdhouse book (opposite).

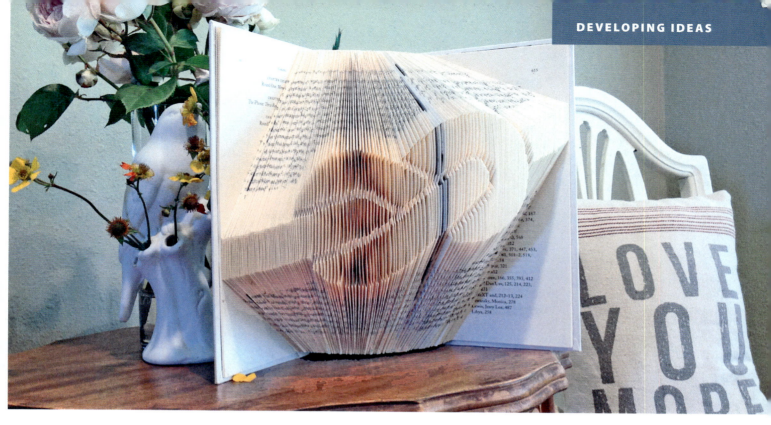

DEVELOPING IDEAS

PERSONALIZING

Birthdays, anniversaries, graduations, and pretty much any holidays that revolve around gift giving are perfect occasions for folding personalized books.

Here are some ideas, but don't let these limit your imagination:

- First name or initials
- Signature
- The shape of someone's home state with a heart inside
- Logo of a favorite team, music band, or superhero
- A comforting phrase for someone suffering loss

COMMEMORATING

One of the most requested custom patterns in my Etsy shop are dates. These can be folded as gifts or as display pieces for parties celebrating special occasions.

Here are some examples to get your imagination going:

- Birth date
- Engagement date
- Graduation date
- Wedding date
- Book publishing date
- Solo flight date

DECORATING

Folded books look great as decorative pieces on mantles, dressers, desks, pianos, and more. Use them for parties, holidays, or anytime. Choose a pattern for:

- An inspirational word
- A simple shape, like a heart, star, or paw print
- A holiday-themed word or image
- Sculptural designs
- Political slogan

 Use a folded book to convey a special message, like "Prom?" or "Marry me?"

SELLING

There is a market for handmade, personalized gifts. If you look on Etsy.com, you will find many people are successfully selling their folded book arts. Holiday craft sales can also be good venues for selling folded books.

Start your projects a couple months ahead of the major commemorative dates so you have time to market them.

Use any of the themes already listed.

DEVELOPING IDEAS

ANNA MOOS

Consider a play on words and symbols, then order a custom pattern. This sculpted book plays on the photographer's last name "Moos" with a moose antler as the M

THINGS TO THINK ABOUT

There are no blank spaces in book folding. Because of this, you get to be creative in putting together two or more words.

Here are some options:

• Do sets of books, e.g., fold three books that say "Welcome home Dad" or two books with "Marry Me?"

• Use different fonts for two or more words strung together in a single book

• Offset two or more words. Place one word slightly above another word so there is a visual separation without an actual space.

• Put a dot, dash, or small heart between words or numbers

• Add a bar that spans the entire set of words or letters from left to right. Add the bar above, below, or straight through the pattern (as in "Mangia" to the right)

DEVELOPING IDEAS

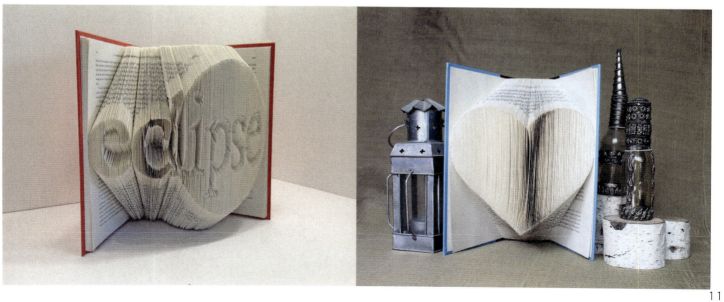

the Right Book

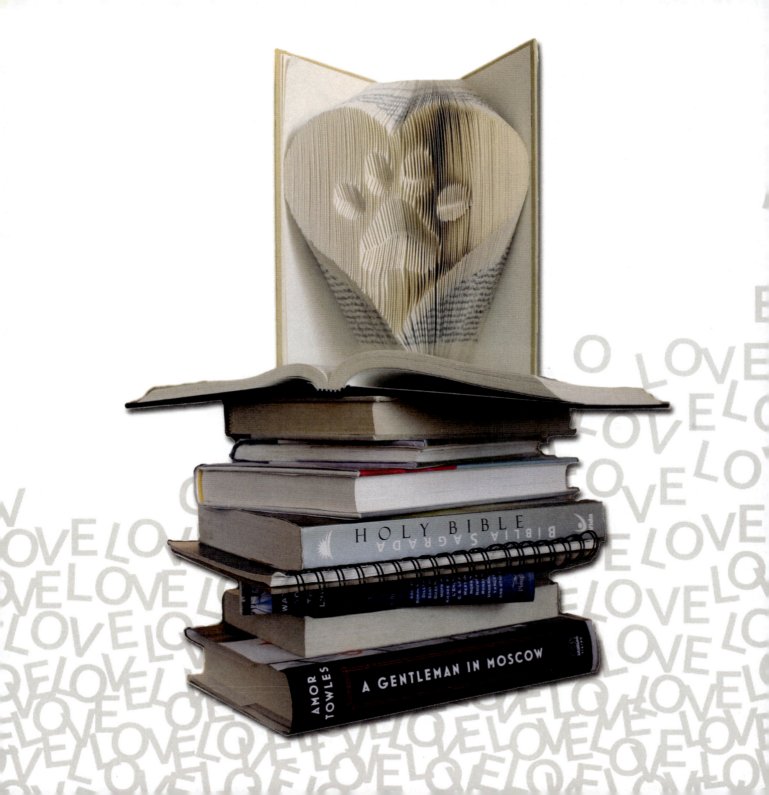

THE RIGHT BOOK

Picking the Right Book

When you read, you begin with A B C. When you do book-folding, you begin with the right book. Sometimes you start with a book you already have in mind and look for a pattern that will work with the book, and sometimes you will have a particular image, word or message in mind and need to find a suitable book for it. Either way, there are certain basic requirements for book folding books.

Often, the content of the book itself is part of the craft. But aside from the topic, you will want to find a book that will make your job of folding easier rather than nearly impossible; that will show your final work crisply; and that will stand up after you're done folding it.

In this section, I will cover the elements needed for the type of cover, the type of paper, and book size.

Knowing what you need before you buy your book will make the project so much easier to complete.

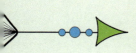 **Think of your project as offering a no-kill option for a good book destined for the rubbish pile by giving it a final purpose.**

The ideal book will have:

- A hard cover
- Pages that aren't old and cracked
- Leaves that aren't too light or too heavy
- A smooth front trim
- Enough pages for your pattern.
- Height of at least 9.5 inches and width of at least 6 inches

THE RIGHT BOOK

BOOK COVERS

Book folding always requires a hard cover book.

Why a hard cover? Because the book will need legs to stand on once it's folded. When you fold a book, you take all support away from the bottom edge of the book, so if it has a soft cover, the book will topple forward. Your book will also spread open once it's folded, making it even more likely to topple forward if it doesn't have a sturdy cover.

FRONT EDGES

Some books have unevenly trimmed pages on the front (deckle-edge). Though the uneven trim can look cool on its own, it can ruin your pattern—as you can see in the "Moos" folded book (next page).

The front of your book should be smooth and free of ripples. Notice the difference between the uneven "Moos" pattern and the crisp edges of the "C" pattern (next page).

PAPER QUALITY

The quality of the pages in a book is a matter of preference. With experience, you will find what kinds of paper fold easier and hold nicer, crisper edges.

Try to stay away from ancient manuscripts, as the pages will split and tear in places that you don't want.

Also, avoid pages that are too thin (such as a Bible) or too thick (photo books).

NUMBER OF PAGES

Generally speaking, the more pages a pattern uses, the more detailed and crisp the final outcome. Pages in a book are like pixels in an image: the more pixels, the easier on the eyes.

Pre-made patterns will tell you how many pages to use. For custom patterns, your designer will give you a range of pages for the desired pattern, and you will then get to choose a book to fit that pattern.

Deckle Edge

Use an uneven front trim (deckle-edge) if you have no other choice, but know that you will have to trim the most obvious stand-out sheets with a blade or scissors for your pattern to show clearly

THE RIGHT BOOK

Smooth Trim

Book folding is not a perfect science and should not look machine made. But you do want the pattern to be recognizable, and the better the paper and trim quality, the easier it will be to show off your workmanship

For uneven-trim books, the pattern can get lost in the jagged front edges. You may have to manually clean up (cut) the uneven front trim, so it's best to use a book with a smooth front trim to begin with.

Imperfection can look cool, but it shouldn't completely hide your image.

The image to the right shows a close-up of my "Moos" book before trimming. The stand-out edges were so distracting, I had to cut the most obvious ones down to smooth out the final image.

Deckle-edge for me? Never again!

 Though Dollar Store books are not always the best in paper quality, they are in the acceptable range, and since most of them have hard covers and cost only $1, they make ideal books.

THE RIGHT BOOK

Can you tell this pattern is a capital T?
Hint: avoid using books full of colored images

How Many Pages?

THE RIGHT BOOK

WORDS AND NUMBERS

There is no straightforward answer to the question of how many pages you will *need* for a folded book. The simplest answer is **"the more, the better."**

Pages in a book are like pixels in an image: the more pixels, the easier on the eyes. When talking about a book, for the same image, the more pages you use, the crisper the design will look.

RULE OF THUMB:

So even though there isn't an exact answer to the question, I have my own rules of thumb for book folding.

These include:

- About 100 numbered pages (50 sheets), for a lower case letter or number
- About 150 numbered pages (75 sheets) for an upper-case letter in a word (not an initial)
- At least 300 pages (150 sheets) for a simple initial and 400 pages for a fancy initial or monogram

There are exceptions: you will use more for "m" and "w," and fewer pages for "i" and "j," etc.

For example, if you wanted to fold the word "Love," you would want a book with around 450 numbered pages (give or take 20 pages): 150 pages for "L" and 100 pages each for "o," "v," and "e."

The above is true if you're using a plain font. Fancier fonts with more details will require more pages per letter. Why? The same reason a photo with more details will need more pixels to render the image well.

MONOGRAMS

If you want to fold an entire book with one or two initials, the rule of thumb is at least 300 numbered pages (150 sheets) for a simple font and at least 400 pages (200 sheets) for a fancy font.

Again, take into account that you will need fewer pages for letters such as I and J, and more for M and W.

at least 300 pages

at least 400 pages

✱ **Height.** Since most books are in the 8 to 10 inches tall range, most patterns are made for that size book. A good size book is around 9.5 inches tall and 6 inches wide (or deep, depending on how you're looking at the book).

You can get custom patterns or learn to make your own for smaller (or larger) books, but the smaller the book, the harder it is to fold a good word or image.

AT LEAST 800 PAGES

PICTURES

It's difficult to come up with a precise rule of thumb for folded pictures. You can make a simple heart or circle shape with as few as 150 pages (75 sheets), but the more detail your image has beyond a simple block figure, the more pages you will absolutely need to make your design come to life.

In the picture of the two hearts with paws to the right, the first book uses 318 pages and the second one uses 446 pages. See how much smoother the second heart looks? The illusion of a paw print works in both books, but the pattern looks *better* with more pages.

You cannot fold an image of a man galloping on horseback in a 300 page book.

Fortunately, most projects are made using premade patterns, and those patterns will tell you exactly how many pages they require. Then you get to find a book to fit the pattern.

When using a custom pattern, the pattern maker will be able to advise you on page numbers once you explain the image you have in mind. Then you can either revise your image to fit the book you want, or find a more appropriate book for the degree of detail in your custom image.

FORGET IT

THE RIGHT BOOK

Each sheet of paper in a book has two numbers—one on the front and one on the back. A book with 100 sheets of paper will have 200 "numbered pages"

The two books shown here used the same "heart with dog paw" pattern except that one pattern was made for almost twice as many pages as the other.

What differences do you see? Would you give either one to a friend? Which would you be proudest to display? Why?

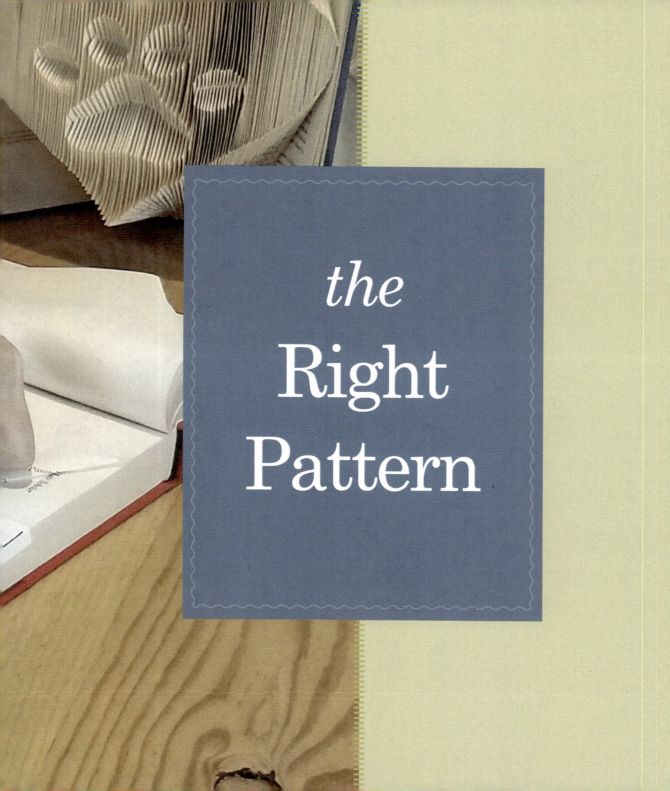

the Right Pattern

THE RIGHT PATTERN

Finding a Pattern

Now that you have the right book, the next step is to find your pattern. Patterns can be bought ready-made or ordered custom-made online. You can also make your own pattern if you have the patience and time to learn.

There are two types of patterns commonly used: the measure-and-mark kind, and the striped image pattern. The measure-and-mark variety have been around for quite some time, while the striped image variety is a simplified pattern using a more intuitive and faster method.

Both these types of patterns are printed out on a sheet of paper for use.

There is a third way to make a pattern, and that is to draw or write your pattern directly onto the front of the closed book. I have never seen a successful result using this "pattern," so it will not be discussed further in this book.

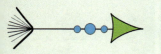

You can find all kinds of patterns with slight price differences between sellers on Etsy.com

Measure-and-Mark Patterns

There are two kinds of folding methods, and therefore two kinds of patterns. The most common folding method is the measure-and-mark method. The pattern for this method is a long list of numbers in two columns. Actually, it's a long list of numbers in 3 columns: page number, top mark, bottom mark.

Each row in the list corresponds either to a numbered page in the book or to the "leaf" number. Because each sheet (leaf) of paper in a book has a number on the front and back, this pattern may use either. If using the page numbers as they are in a book, you will only see odd numbers (the front of the page).

If the pattern goes by leaves of paper, then it will list each leaf (or sheet) as 1, 2, 3, 4, etc.

For each page, you get two numbers. You will measure down to the first number (in inches or centimeters) and mark, then measure to the second number and mark.

You then fold—either using the 90 degree method or the same marked point along the top and bottom of the book for all pages (we will come to this later).

Page 1	7.7	8.9
Page 3	7.1	9.6
Page 5	6.8	10.1
Page 7	6.6	10.5
Page 9	6.4	10.9
Page 11	6.3	11.2
Page 13	6.2	11.6
Page 15	6.1	11.8
Page 17	6.0	12.1
Page 19	6.0	12.4
Page 21	6.0	12.6
Page 23	6.0	12.8
Page 25	6.0	13.1

THE RIGHT PATTERN

WHEN BUYING A PATTERN remember that each sheet of paper in a book has two numbers—one on the front and one on the back. A 200-page book will have 100 sheets (or "leaves") of paper. Be sure to check with the pattern maker if the number on the pattern refers to the number of leaves or page numbers.

Striped Patterns

The second, and I think easier, book folding method is to follow a striped pattern. The pattern is inserted behind the page you are going to fold and you simply fold back to the top and bottom of the stripe for that page.

In the fold-only method, parts of broken stripes are ignored and the final image is a perfect illusion of the printed pattern.

In the cut-and-fold method, each section of each stripe is folded, rendering a more detailed look.

The upside for using striped patterns is that it is faster than following a long list of numbers.

The down side is that you have to pay closer attention to the pattern and which stripe you're on rather than just follow the numbers given to you.

Also, the stripes can start to swim in your vision, so you need occasional breaks while folding your book.

Ready-Made Books

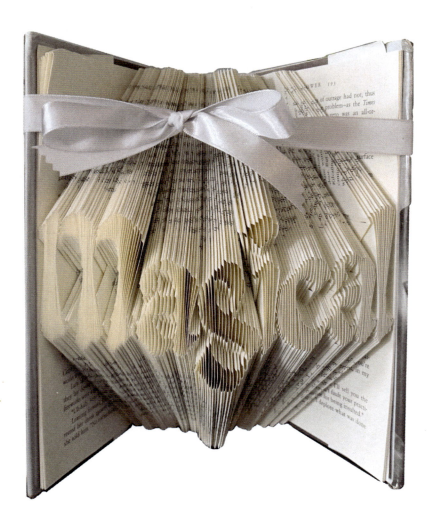

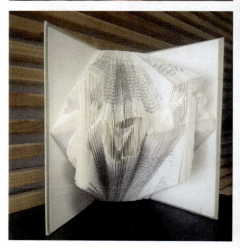

Did you know you can order books that are already folded with your custom request? Check out www.etsy.com/shop/JoJosReticules and other shops on Etsy

Ready-Made Patterns

Ready-made patterns range from simple generic hearts and holiday-themed designs to whimsical phrases and images.

Patterns can be found in various places on the Internet--some even for free--but Etsy is probably the best single source for the greatest variety of patterns.

When purchasing a ready-made pattern, you will need to consider the number of pages *in the pattern* when selecting your book. Since it is nearly impossible to find books that exactly match the number of pages in ready-made patterns, you will need a book with more pages than are in the pattern. This will leave you with left-over pages which should be divided equally between the front and back of the pattern.

THE RIGHT PATTERN

dobra para tras / fold back

usa 400 paginas / uses 400 pages

Custom Patterns

The advantage of a custom pattern is that you can create something unique and specific to your wants, and have it made to fit the number of pages in your book so you don't have large sections of unfolded pages before and after your pattern.

Just remember from the previous section on "The Right Book" that there are some basic requirements for page numbers depending on the complexity of your pattern. You cannot order a custom pattern for the phrase "MarryMe" if you want to use a special book with only 250 pages.

When ordering a custom pattern, you and the seller will have to communicate back and forth about the intended word or image and page number needs before completing a transaction.

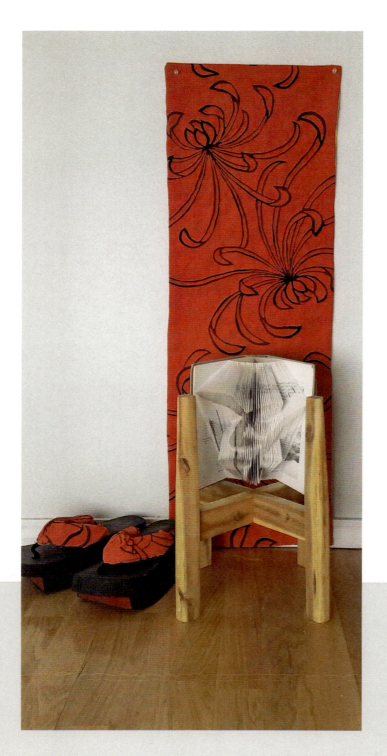

Above: Kanji for "peace."
Left: I can't for the life of me remember what the kanji in the photo at left stands for. Anyone know and care to share?

THE RIGHT PATTERN

how to Fold a Book

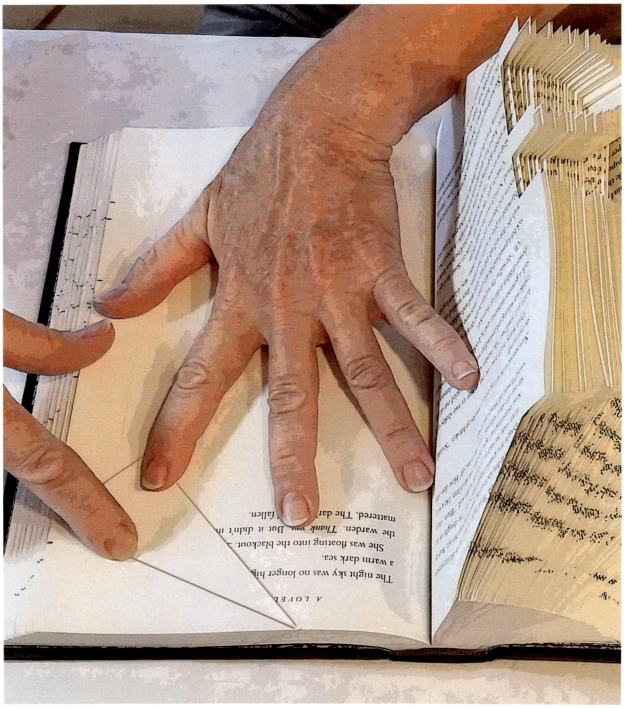

HOW TO FOLD

Folding a Book

Enough talk about book requirements and pattern types. It's time to learn how to actually fold your pattern into a book. Welcome at last to the step by step instructions.

In this chapter we will cover every question including, where do you sit? Do you need tools? Is there anything you need to do to the book first? What size is the pattern? How do you use it? And more.

By the end of this chapter you will be mentally ready to tackle the most important chapter: putting what you learned into practice.

We will look at the two main variations in book folding methods: "fold-only" (standard fold) and "cut-and-fold," and then briefly discuss some further variations under each of these.

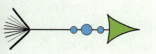 **Take a breath. You're about to learn a beautiful and practical art form!**

Before you start

LOCATION

You can do book folding almost anywhere:
- **At a dining table**
- **At a tall kitchen Island**
- **At a low coffee table**
- **In the car**

For beginners, I would start at a table where you can have ready access to your tools at all times. The more you practice, the less you will need tools, but beginners will find them helpful.

LIGHTING

You will need very good lighting for book folding. The best light is natural light--and lots of it. If you can sit outdoors out of direct sunlight but in a well-lit area, do so. You don't want to be blinded, but every bit of light will help to see the fine lines of your pattern and the pencil marks on your book.

If you can't sit outdoors, make sure there is spot lighting on your project.

SEATING (OR NOT)

Because you will be leaning forward with both arms reaching in front of you, you will need to settle into a comfortable position while book folding.

Experiment with what works for you: a straight-back chair at a dining table; standing at a tall counter; sitting on a couch by a coffee table; etc.

Wherever you settle, get up and stretch every so often.

TOOLS

There are some essential and optional tools for your project:

Essential:
- **a sharp, rigid tool**
- **a sharp pencil or pen**

Optional:
- **a straight edge**
- **a paper creaser**
- **a colored pencil or pen**
- **scissors**
- **reading glasses**
- **an anti-skid mat**

HOW TO FOLD

Preparing your book

1. Draw a guide line about two inches from the spine on the bottom of the book.
2. Do the same for the top of the book, then gouge out the top line with a sharp object such as an ice pick or galvanized nail.

Picture the setting: you are sitting at a table with the book on the table in front of you. You can see the bottom of the book, but not the top. You need to draw a line on the bottom and top of the book that you will use to guide your folds. The line on the bottom of the book will be plainly visible while you work. But what about the top of the book? If you simply draw a line across the pages at the top, you won't be able to see the line without flipping the top towards you. This won't do when you're working on your pattern. The solution is to draw a line across the top and then score it with a sharp object. That way, when you open your book, every page will have a tiny tic mark (or indentation) where you gouged out the line.

The line at the bottom and the tic marks at the top will be your guides while folding your book.

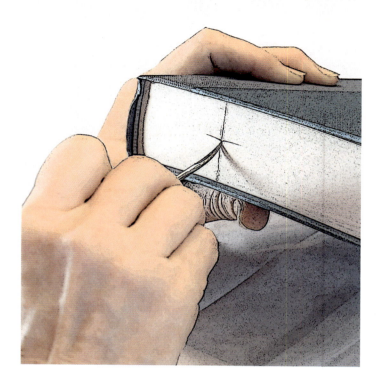

HOW TO FOLD

← draw a line

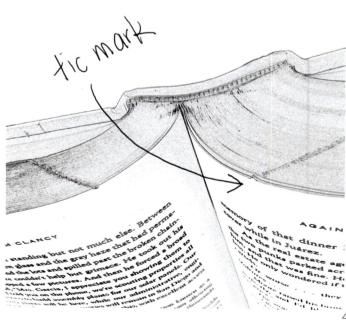

tic mark

Folding your book (standard fold)

The following instructions are for striped image patterns.

The striped pattern is used behind the page you are going to fold. Each stripe--**both black and white**--corresponds to one page of your book.

The tab at the top of the pattern ensures that your folds line up all the way through the pattern.

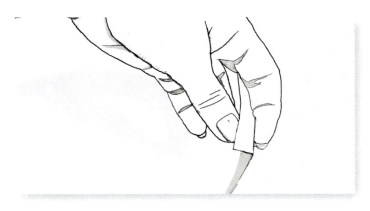

STEP 1
Fold the pattern back at the top line to form a tab

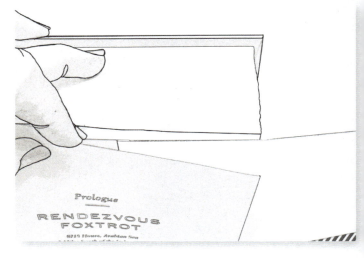

STEP 2
Hook the pattern to the page behind the one you are going to fold

You can also leave the tab hanging out but hooked to the top of the book behind the page you are going to fold. Be sure to tap the pattern flush with the top of the book before marking your book.

HOW TO FOLD

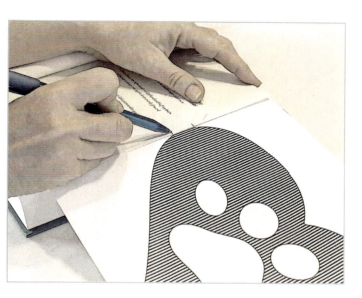

STEP 3

Slide the pattern behind the page you are going to fold until the fist stripe lines up with the edge of the page

STEP 4

Mark the top and bottom of the stripe on the book page with a fine-tip pen or pencil. Note: once you get enough experience, you can skip this step and make your folds without marking the book page. Use a straight edge (a ruler or a piece of mat board) to line up the folds as you see in the images to the right.

> As a beginner you will need to mark the top and bottom of the stripe that corresponds to each page, but with practice you will be able to fold without ever marking your book.

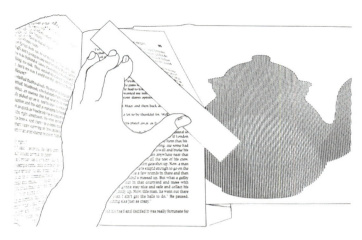

STEP 5

Using a straight edge, line up the top mark with the tic mark at the top of the book. Fold the top edge of the page towards you. Crease the fold with your thumb or bone folder

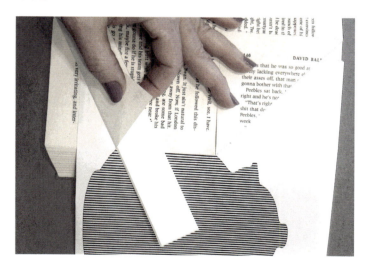

STEP 6

Repeat step 5 with the bottom marks (bottom of stripe and bottom of book)

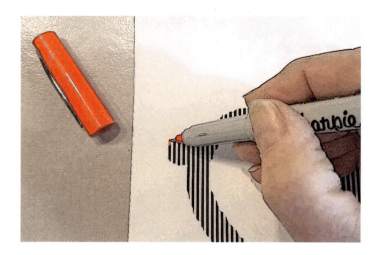

STEP 7

Mark the stripe you just folded to keep track of where you are on the pattern. You don't have to use a colored pen, but it helps to make it stand out against the black and white stripes

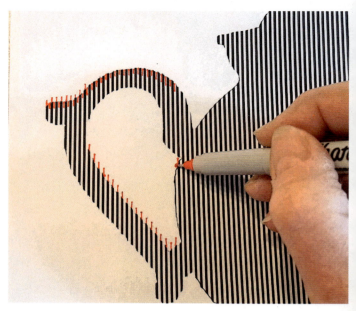

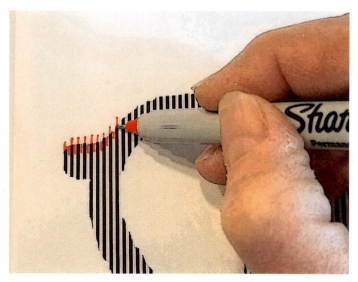

STEP 8

Continue folding each page and marking each unbroken stripe--both black and white--until you come to a broken stripe.

STEP 9

When you reach a broken stripe, fold the *top* section of the stripe, mark it, then move to the next stripe and fold the *next level down* and mark it.

Any time your stripes are broken into sections, follow this simple rule: always move one stripe forward and one level down as you go. *Never fold more than one section of a single vertical stripe.*

In this method of book folding, you are creating an illusion. Each stripe represents one page of the book. If a stripe is broken, you will fold only one section of that stripe and skip to the next stripe.

In the teapot handle above, the first broken stripe is white. I folded the top of the broken white stripe, turned the page folded the bottom of the black stripe, turned the page, folded the top of the next white stripe, turned the page, folded the bottom of the next black stripe, etc.

Continue folding your pattern this way until you are done.

You have now successfully learned to fold a book without cutting any pages.

HOW TO FOLD

This teapot accidentally turned out two-tone. It just so happened that most of the illustrations in the book were on the top half of the page.

Variations in folding methods

standard fold

90 degree fold

STANDARD FOLD

As a review, the standard way to fold a book is to mark the top and bottom a couple inches from the spine and fold every page to the same point at top and bottom.

There will be minor variations in the top fold, as it is nearly impossible to get all folds to match the tic mark exactly.

Since the front of the book is the main point of the pattern, there is no need to worry about small errors at the top and bottom.

90 DEGREE FOLD

Another way to fold back each page is to use a straight angle, making each fold at a 45 degree angle (see above, right).

There is no need to mark the top and bottom of your book if you are folding at a 45 degree angle all the way through the book.

This method creates an interesting alternate design, echoing the pattern at the top and bottom of the book, as you can see in the "eclipse" book above.

SKIP A PAGE

In the three hearts to the right, there are three different effects created using the same pattern.

The first heart is folded the same as the middle heart except that it skips every 5th page. This method gives an almost hidden effect to your pattern.

When to skip a page will depend on the length of your book versus the pattern. Divide the pattern pages by the leftover pages and that will be your skipped page number.

SKIP AND FOLD

The third heart in the image to the right also skips every few pages, but this time the skipped page is folded back a couple inches straight up and down.

The effect of skipping and folding creates a similar effect to the cut-and-fold method without increasing the amount of work. The pattern will appear to stand out against a slightly recessed background.

HOW TO FOLD

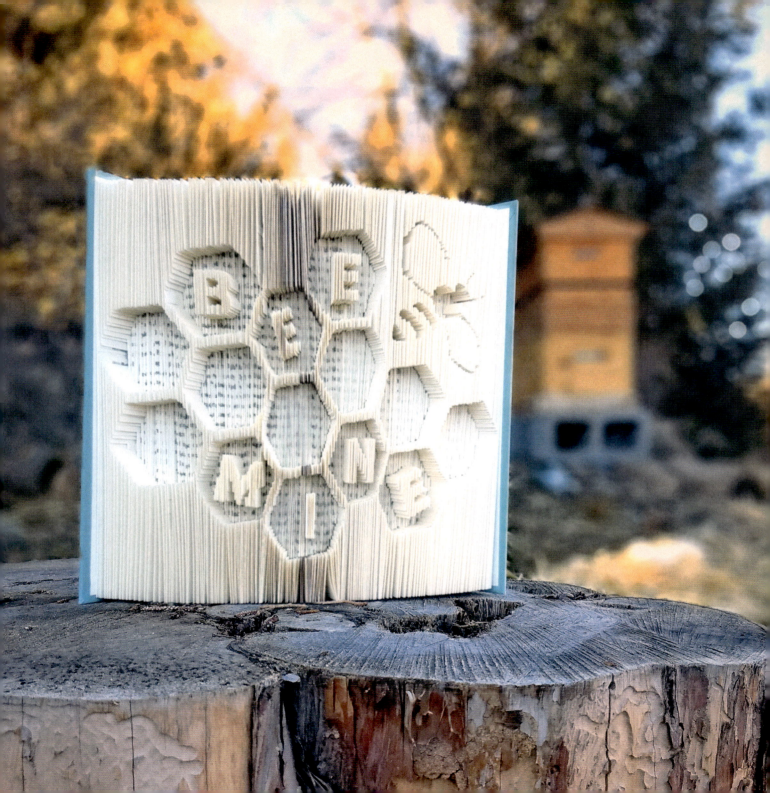

What about Cut and Fold?

HOW TO FOLD

In the image on the next 2-page spread there are two books folded to the same pattern (Moos) with the same number of pages. The one on the left is folded without cutting, and the one on the right follows the cut-and-fold method.

Notice how much more detailed the cut-and-fold book looks? That is because in the "fold-only" variation, there are only two folds for every page, leaving bits of the design unfolded. But in cut-and-fold, you fold every piece of every single stripe, even if the stripe is broken into 10 pieces.

The cut-and-fold method will take four or five times longer to complete, but the payoff is great if you have the time for it.

In the practice section of this book, we will use the faster method of using a striped pattern to fold an image without cutting any pages.

But on the next page here I will give you the steps to the cut-and-fold method which you can use with any striped pattern.

Cut-and-fold is actually a simpler method to follow and generally gives you a more detailed result. But it will consume much more of your time than the no-cut method, so consider yourself forewarned.

These two books are folded using the same pattern and number of pages. The first uses the standard fold method and the second uses the cut-and-fold method. Sometimes the difference is striking, but not always. In this case, the first book also had an uneven front trim which threw off the pattern

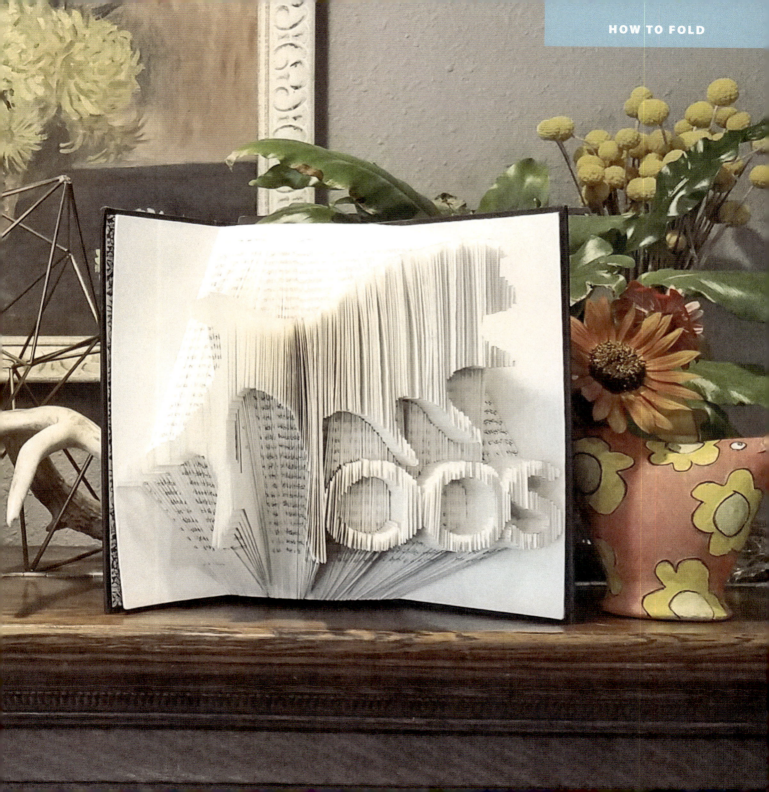

HOW TO FOLD

Cut-and-fold with a striped pattern:

STEP 1

Fold your pattern back at the top to form a tab

STEP 2

Open your book to the first page of the project. Insert the pattern behind the page you are going to mark and hook it snugly to the top of the book. Slide the pattern out until the first stripe meets the edge of the book.

Mark the top and bottom of the stripe directly onto the book page. If the stripe is broken into sections, mark the top and bottom of every section of that stripe onto the book page

Turn the page and repeat with the next stripe. Mark both black and white stripes (each stripe represents one page in your book)

HOW TO FOLD

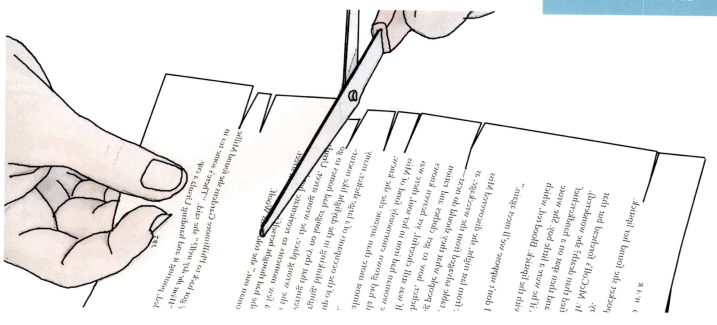

STEP 3

When you are done marking up the whole pattern, go back to the first page and cut all marks to the edge of the text on that page. If there is no text, cut to where the text would be

STEP 4

When you are done cutting the whole book, go back and fold each page. Fold the first tab back, then fold every other tab back as shown below.

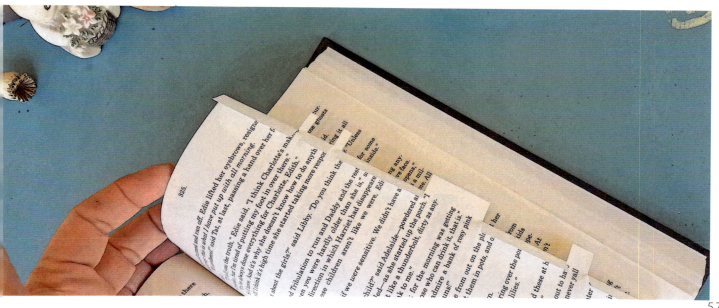

57

Variations in Cut-and-Fold

PATTERN PROTRUDING FROM THE BOOK

Step 4 on the previous page instructs you to fold the first tab back, then fold *every other* tab back.

This method will make your pattern stand out from the rest of the book pages like the Moos book. Normally, the pattern will stand out against a flat background.

The Moos book below stands out against an angled background. See the third variation on how to do this.

PATTERN RECEDING INTO THE BOOK

To make your pattern recede (sink into) the front of the book, you will skip the first tab, then fold every other tab back in step 4.

There is no need to prepare your book for folding as instructed in the standard method of folding. The first and last tabs will not be folded back at an angle.

The result is an image that will look almost burned deep into the flat surface of the book.

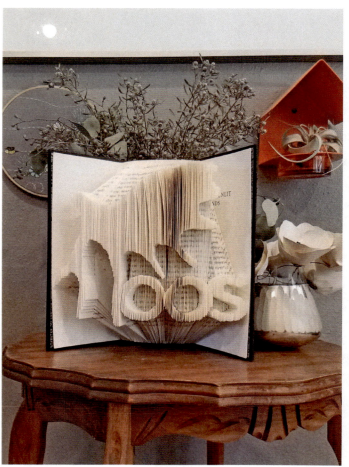

HOW TO FOLD

ANGLED TOP AND BOTTOM

To achieve an angled top and bottom in a cut-and-fold book, you will prepare your book for folding the same way you prepare a standard-fold book as instructed on page 49.

You will cut every mark you made on the book, and then you will fold the first tab back to the tic mark at the top of your book at an angle.

Every other tab is folded straight back, then the bottom tab is also folded at an angle to the tic mark at the bottom of the book (example above).

The advantage of folding the top and bottom at an angle is that the pages will fan out as they do in the standard fold method.

Notice the difference between the two cut and fold books on the previous page. The Moos pattern fans open while the nativity image looks more smooshed together. I had to insert scraps of paper between the nativity pages to fan it out more.

Cut and fold images can look smooshed unless you add angled folds at the top and bottom of the page

COMBINATION FOLD

The heart with a rose inside (above) is an example of a combination of the standard fold and cut-and-fold methods. In this variation, the first and last marks on the page are NOT cut. When it comes to folding, the first and last folds are done at an angle as in the standard method of folding, and then the rose is folded in the cut-and-fold method.

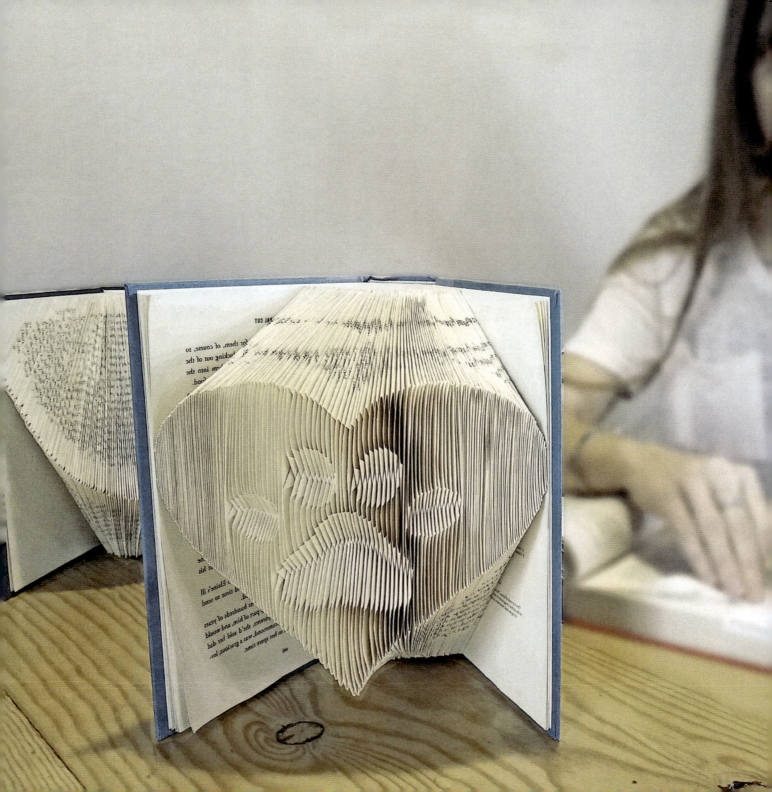

Now *let's* Practice

LET'S PRACTICE

Practice Session

Now you have your book and your pattern. It's time to fold your book!

At the back of this book you will find a pattern for a heart with a dog paw print inside. You are going to use this pattern to learn how to use striped book-folding patterns, moving from easy to more difficult within the same pattern.

When you're done with this pattern, you will be able to fold any striped pattern with any level of difficulty.

This tutorial will follow the standard fold method. If you want, you can follow the cut-and-fold method laid out in the previous chapter. There are no "levels of difficulty" in the cut and fold method, but it will take longer to finish.

Ready?

Let's go!

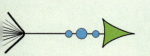 **Don't be afraid of imperfections. As with any other art form, practice makes perfect!**

WHAT YOU'LL NEED:

- A hard cover book with at least 418 numbered pages
- A mechanical pencil or fine-tipped pen
- A sharp object such as an ice pick
- A straight edge (ruler or piece of card stock)
- A colored pencil (something that will stand out from the black and white stripes)
- A paper creaser to make your folds crisper (optional)

Prepare your book

LET'S PRACTICE

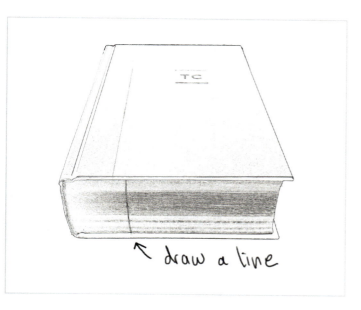

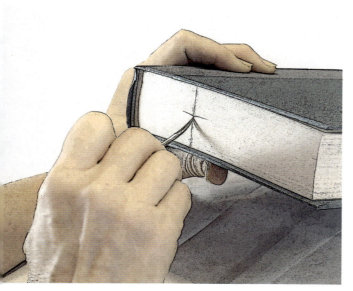

STEP 1

Draw a line across the top of the book pages about 2 inches from the spine with a pen or pencil.

STEP 2

Draw another line on the bottom of the book about 2 inches from the spine with a pen or pencil.

STEP 3

Gouge out (score deeply) the top line with a sharp object such as an ice pick. This gouge needs to be deep enough to make a small tic mark on every page when you set the book down and open it up. Since the marking on the top of the book will be out of sight when you're folding your book, you need a way to see where that line is. The indented tic mark will be your guide.

You do not need to gouge out the line on the bottom of the book since you will be able to see it from where you're sitting while you're making your folds.

STEP 4

Count how many pages you have over the needed 418 numbered pages. Divide that number in two. Mark your beginning page. For example, if you have 100 pages left over, mark page number 50 as your starting point.

Prepare your pattern

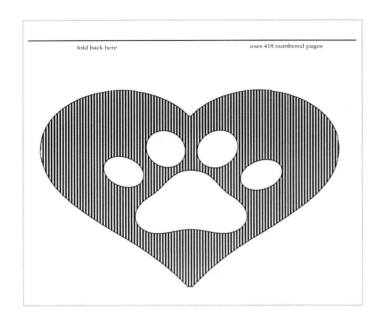

STEP 1

Cut the Heart-with-Paw pattern out of the back of this instruction book and photocopy it onto a regular 8.5 x 11 sheet of paper in landscape orientation. Make sure that the pattern is straight! Your stripes must be perfectly vertical and not slanted for this to work. Save the original pattern so you have something to copy next time.

STEP 2

Fold the top of the pattern back at the line as shown. If the line doesn't show, fold about 1/4 inch straight across from the top. This will form a tab that hooks onto the top of the book pages and keeps the pattern even from beginning to end.

LET'S PRACTICE

EXPLAINING PATTERN SECTIONS

I chose this paw print heart for our exercise because it is a perfect example of moving from easy to more complex within a single pattern.

I split the pattern into sections to better explain.

Notice that the first section of this pattern has no broken stripes. This is what I call a "solid pattern." If this heart did not have a paw print inside, the whole pattern would be "solid."

Solid patterns are the easiest kind of pattern to fold (whether you are doing standard or cut-and-fold).

The second section of this paw print heart has stripes broken into two pieces. This is still easy, but requires a little more focus when folding.

The third section has stripes that are broken into more than two sections. The more a pattern is broken up like this, the more you will have to pay close attention to what stripe you are folding.

Marking off your progress with a colored pen or pencil will help you keep track of where you are along the way.

Remember that every stripe corresponds to one page in your book. If you fold multiple pieces of a single stripe on different pages, you will quickly run out of pages.

First Section: Folding Solid Patterns

The first part of this exercise is a solid pattern. The solid part of this pattern uses 88 numbered pages (44 sheets).

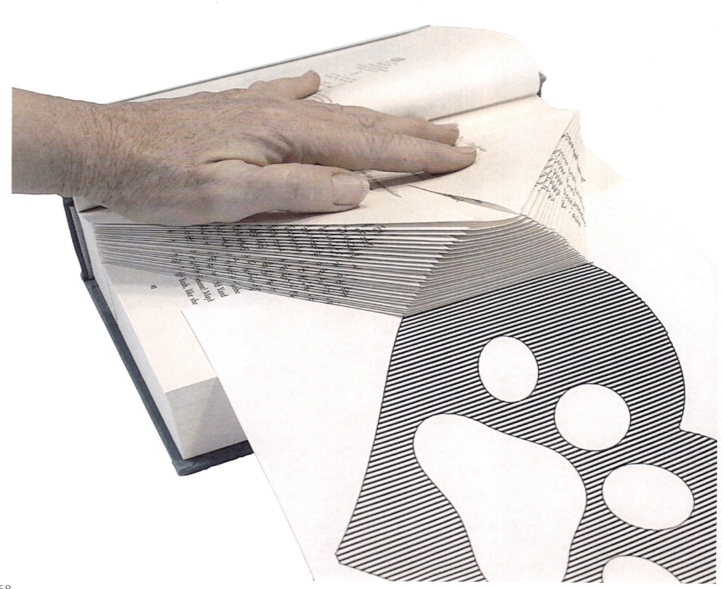

LET'S PRACTICE

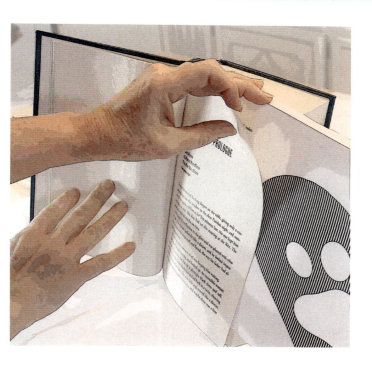

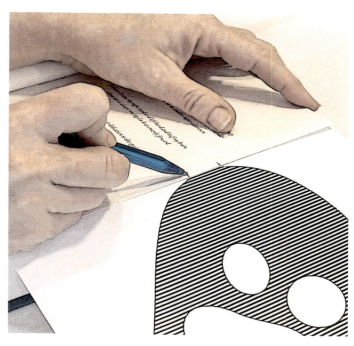

STEP 1

Place the practice pattern behind the first page of your book with the tab hooked onto the top of the book.

Slide the pattern behind the page until the first stripe touches the outside edge of the page. Make sure the top tab is flush against the top of the book.

STEP 2

Mark the top and bottom of the stripe onto the book page with a fine-tipped pen or pencil.

STEP 3 (STANDARD FOLD)

If you're folding all pages to the same place top and bottom, the first fold goes from the top mark you just made to the notch you carved at the top of the book. The second fold goes from the bottom mark you just made to the line you marked at the bottom of the book.

STEP 3 (45 DEGREE FOLD)

Remember that the previous steps can be made with a 45-degree fold instead of the standard fold. If you are using this alternate method, make both the top and bottom folds using a triangle guide.

LET'S PRACTICE

STEP 4

Once both folds are made, draw a tic mark with a colored pen or pencil on the stripe you folded to keep track of your progress. Using a color other than black helps you to see the tic marks better.

STEP 5

Go on to the next page and the next stripe (black) and repeat the above instructions. Continue on with the pattern until you reach the first paw print circle.

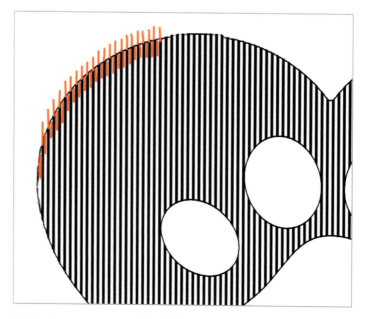

This is what your pattern will look like after you have folded each stripe to this point and marked your place with a red pen.

71

CHECK YOUR WORK: FIRST SECTION

Your pattern so far will have 44 folded sheets of paper which equal 88 numbered pages and should look like this.

Second Section: Folding Two-Level Patterns

The next part of the pattern has two levels. That is, the next 22 stripes are broken in two by the open space created by the dog paw. Since you must never fold more than one page on a single vertical stripe, you will:

STEP 1

Fold the top half of the next stripe (white).

STEP 2

Move one page forward and fold the bottom part of the next stripe (black).

Notice that you are leaving parts of each stripe unfolded. Don't worry. Trust the process. Doing it this way will create the exact illusion of the final image when you're done. If you fold all sections of all stripes, you will run out of pages before you're done, and your image will be stretched out in some sections.

In this section, because you started with the top of a white stripe, you will be folding top white, bottom black, top white, bottom black, etc.

Continue in this manner until you get to page 131/132

CHECK YOUR WORK: SECTION TWO

Your book should now look like this, with 65 folded sheets of paper which equal 130 numbered pages.

The tic marks on your pattern should look like this (see insert)

Third Section: Folding Multi-Level Patterns

LET'S PRACTICE

Notice that the next stripe you come to in the practice pattern is white, and it is cut into three pieces.

Starting on page 133, continue in the same way as you did with stripes broken in two, except that now you will have a top, a middle, and a bottom section.

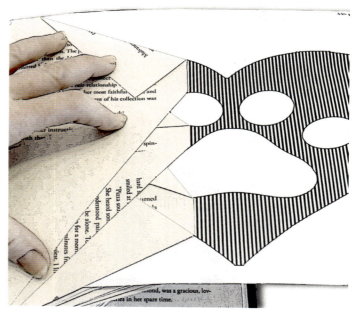

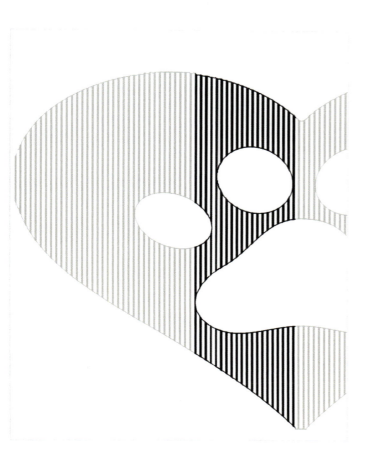

STEP 1

Fold the top part of the next stripe (white n this case)

STEP 2

Move to the next black stripe and fold the middle section

STEP 3

Move to the next white stripe and fold the bottom part, then fold the top part of the next black stripe, and so on.

As long as you keep moving forward to the next stripe and the next level, your pattern will form the image in the folds of the book.

1 stripe = 1 sheet of paper

never fold more than one page on a single vertical stripe

The tic marks on your pattern will look like this

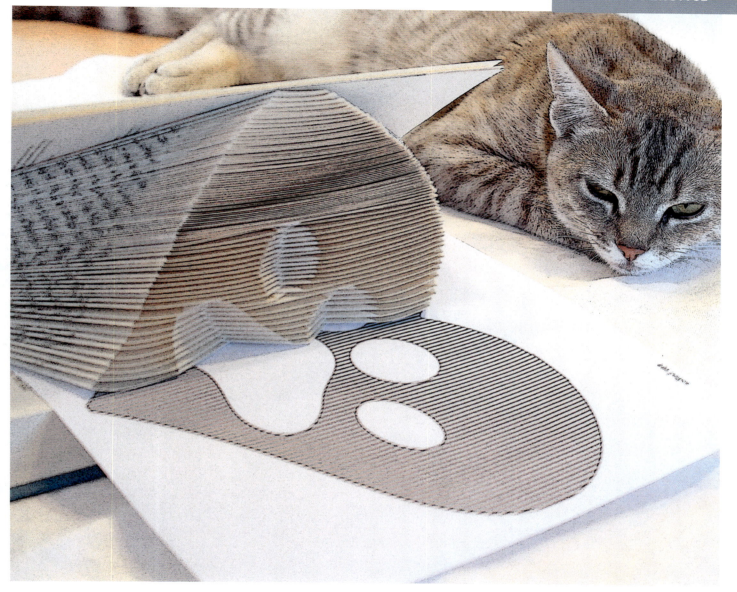

LET'S PRACTICE

CHECK YOUR WORK: SECTION THREE

Halfway through the pattern you should be on page 209/210, and your folded book will look like this (minus the cat)

Finish

Continue folding your paw-in-heart pattern to the end.

You will move in reverse order from a multi-level, to a two-level, to a solid pattern as you continue folding the heart.

Always remember the main rules in the standard method of striped pattern folding: fold both black and white stripes, always move forward one stripe per page, and never fold more than one level on a single stripe.

If you want to try the cut-and-fold method with this pattern, review the instructions on page 56. The main difference will be that you will mark and cut and fold *every section of every stripe on each page*.

Congratulations!

You have now learned to use a multiple-level striped book-folding pattern and are ready to fold books using any pattern with any level of difficulty

Just *for* Fun

DIY Striped Patterns

Just for fun, you can use notebook paper to make geometric patterns. Figure out how many sheets you need to string together to equal the number of pages in your book, then tape them together. Draw straight lines one inch apart and come up with a pattern where your lines intersect with the page lines. Those points will be where you fold your page to.

Draw a single wavy line across the notebook paper for another fun DIY pattern. Experiment and have fun!

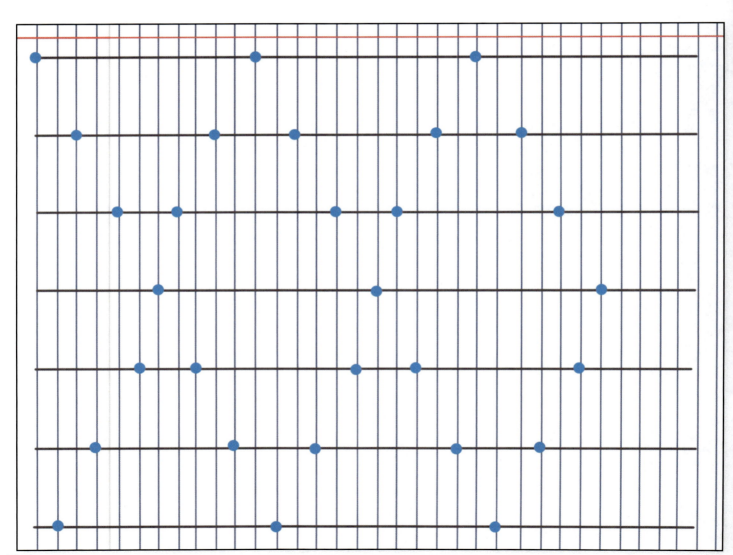

JUST FOR FUN

What do you see? Dragon scales?

83

The Bird House

Use a book with about 150 pages for half a birdhouse. If you want a whole birdhouse, fold a book with 300 pages, rip off the cover, and glue the first and last pages together.

JUST FOR FUN

STEP 1

Fold the top right corner down as shown

STEP 2

Fold the bottom right corner up as shown

STEP 3

Turn the page and fold the top right corner down as shown

STEP 4

Fold the front of the page straight back as shown. Repeat these 4 steps to the end of the book.

Freehand over Striped Backgrounds

If you go to diymarta.com and look for the article titled "Simplified Folded Book Art," you will find several links at the bottom of the article for free striped backgrounds.

Print your striped background in landscape orientation at about 95% of the original size so all the stripes print around the margins.

These striped backgrounds can be used to draw on and create your own custom patterns. You can draw anything from simple geometric shapes--as shown in the illustration on the opposite page--to words, to clipart designs.

You can also insert these striped patterns into your printer and print words or pictures onto them, then use the sheets as patterns for book folding.

Remember that there are no blank spaces in book folding, so you will have to bump your letters together when you design your own pattern.

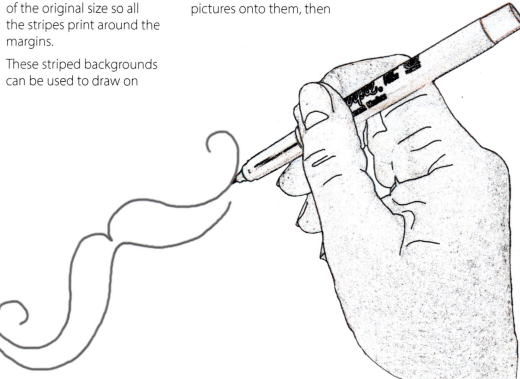

JUST FOR FUN

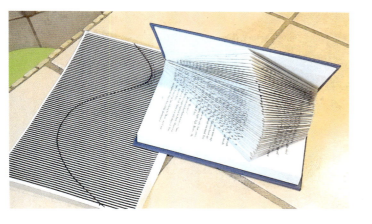

THE WAVE

1. Prepare your book as instructed on page 65 by marking the top and bottom a couple inches from the spine.

2. Draw a wave over a striped background that matches the page number on your book (if there are more pages than stripes, divide the leftover pages by two and start on that page number)

3. Fold each page to the point on each stripe created by your freehand drawing.

Tips *and* Tricks

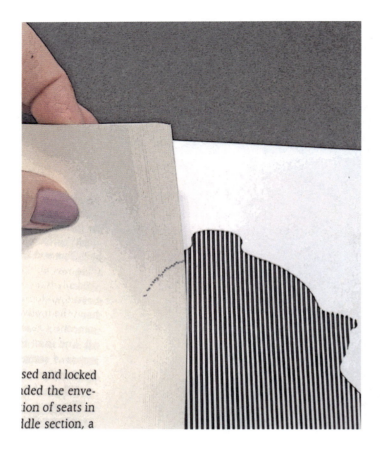

PRE-MARKING THE WHOLE BOOK

Cut-and-fold books are always marked up all the way through before they are cut and folded. But when doing a standard fold book, I usually fold as I go. This means I have to have the pattern with me for the entire project.

I've discovered that it can be practical to mark an entire standard-fold book, then take it with me to fold while I'm waiting in a car or taking a lunch break at work. Marking it up ahead of time means I don't have to deal with the extra paper and pen getting in the way in a tight space.

BULKING UP THE BOOK

One of the benefits of cut-and-fold is that you can use a book with fewer pages to make a more intricate pattern than the standard fold method. The problem that goes with this benefit is that the final project can look too skinny.

You can artificially add openness to your cut-and-fold book by inserting scraps of paper between the pages. This will simulate the fanning that happens with a standard fold book.

You can even insert whole pages in a book that is just shy of the number of pages you need. Do this before you start.

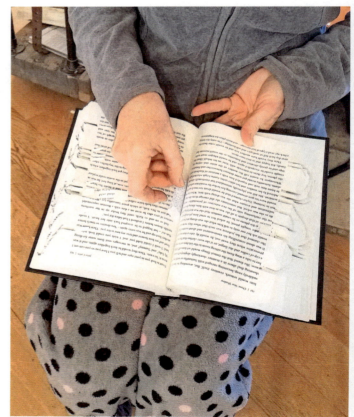

TIPS AND TRICKS

DOG-EARING

With the standard method of book folding, every fold will be at an angle. Sometimes the angle will result in an overlap with the spine of the book.

My work-around is to fold back the tip of the page as shown above. You can also trim it away with scissors.

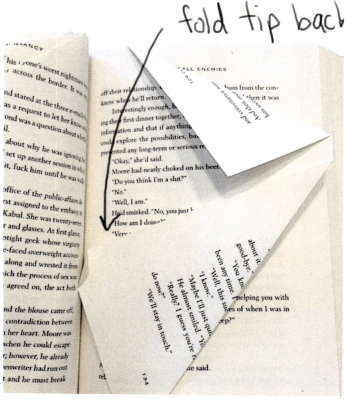

TRIMMING UNEVEN EDGES

In the "Picking the Right Book" section of this book, I strongly advised against using an uneven-trimmed book (deckle edged) because it can make the end result rather messy.

I also shared that if you really must use a book with uneven front trim for, say, sentimental reasons, you can trim away the most obvious stand-out sections with a pair of scissors.

CLIPPING PAGES OUT OF THE WAY

I learned this trick from a student I was teaching. She used a large clip to keep the "done" pages out of the way.

I thought it was so clever, I had to include it here.

KEEPING YOUR WORKING PAGES FLAT

When you are working with a large book (more than 500 pages), your pages will have a curve to them when the book is open flat on the table. The first 200 or so pages of the book won't be a problem, but once you get past the middle, the curve can make it tricky to make a straight fold.

My solution is to stand the front cover up so the section of book I'm working on lays flat. This makes for cleaner, crisper folds.

TIPS AND TRICKS

Fixing mistakes

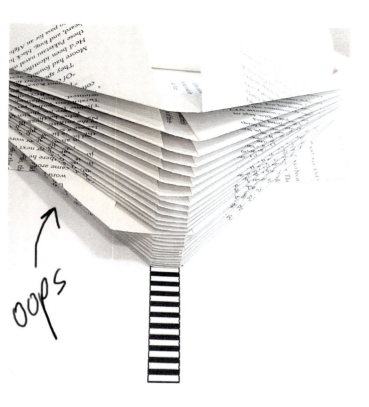

REFOLD

Paper folds have "memories," so you can't completely erase a bad fold. Ideally, the fewer oopses you make, the better your final project will look.

Sometimes, though, a bad fold can really stand out from the work and you know you have to fix it. Fortunately you can fix some mistakes.

To re-fold a bad fold, you will need a hard surface behind it. If you are way past the point that you made the mistake, you can insert a piece of cardboard behind the mistake and simply re-fold it.

If the mistake is minor, leave it alone. Don't let small imperfections keep you from completing your project.

TEAR OUT

What if you lost your place on the pattern and you notice later that you folded several stripes twice?

You can easily fix that mistake by tearing or cutting the pages out of the book. Hopefully you have extra pages at the end of the book to complete your pattern.

INSERT

Suppose on the other hand that you get far into your project and notice that you skipped a few folds by mistake. Or suppose your book is just ten pages shy of the number you need for the pattern?

Just as you can cut out pages, you can insert pages if the need arises.

I suggest simply inserting a page from a different book and trimming it to the size of the book you're working on. Avoid using glue. As long as you insert the page snuggly in between other pages, it should stay put.

REPLACE COVER LINING

If the inner cover does not suit your decor or the theme of your pattern, you can always use a pretty wrapping paper as a replacement inner cover. In this folded birdhouse book., I felt the bright yellow was a distraction from the pattern, so I replaced it with a muted lemon theme paper (below).

TRIMMING AS YOU GO

So you're folding your book, slipping the pattern further and further in behind the page you are going to fold. What do you do when you get to the point where the pattern hits up against the inner spine? Simple. Trim off an inch or two of the pattern when it starts to get in the way.

By the end of my book folding projects, the patterns look like the picture above. Strips of pattern get cut off the further I get into the project.

This is another reason you should not use your original pattern. Set the original aside and make copies to work with.

Patterns

Pattern 1: Heart with Paw Print

This pattern uses 418 numbered pages. Use this pattern for the tutorial on page 65.

Do not use this original sheet. Copy this pattern onto another sheet of paper in landscape orientation. Use the copy to mark off your progress and keep the original for another project.

You can fold with either the conventional or cut-and-fold method.

Optional: if you want to fold a simple heart without a paw, you can use this pattern and simply ignore the paw print as you fold.

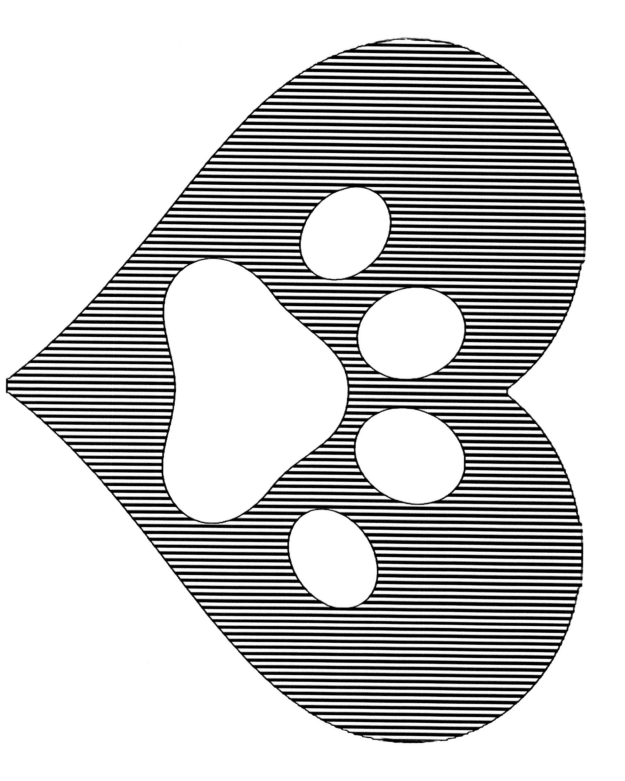

fold back here

uses 418 numbered pages

Pattern 2: Tilted Anchor

Uses 408 numbered pages. Use with either the conventional or cut-and-fold method.

Do not use this original sheet. Copy this pattern onto another sheet of paper in landscape orientation. Use the copy to mark off your progress and keep the original for another project.

fold back here

uses 408 numbered pages

Pattern 3: Be Kind

Uses 350 numbered pages. This pattern should only be used with the cut-and-fold method.

For a recessed look (see previous page), leave the first tab on each page unfolded, then fold back every other tab.

To make the words stand out from the book, fold the first tab back on every page, then fold back every other tab.

Do not use this original sheet. Copy this pattern onto another sheet of paper in landscape orientation. Use the copy to mark off your progress and keep the original for another project.

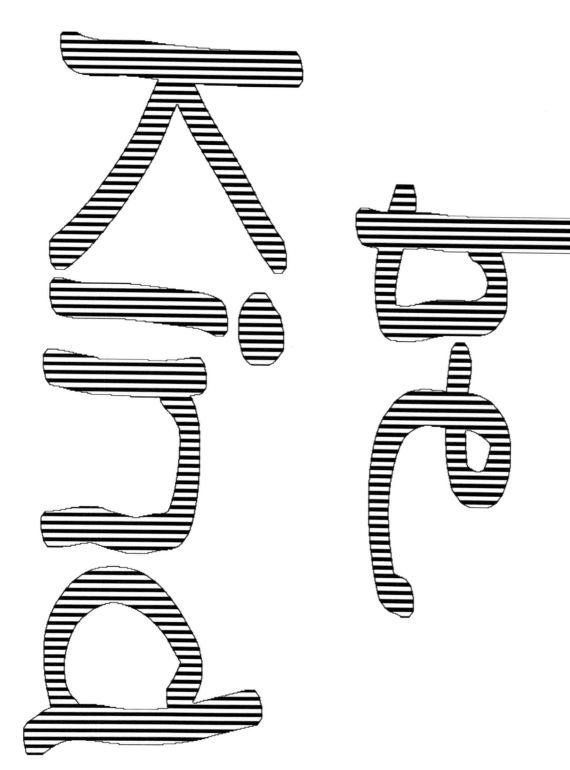

fold back here

uses 350 numbered pages

Pattern 4: Home

Uses 418 numbered pages. This pattern can be folded using either the conventional or cut-and-fold methods.

Do not use this original sheet. Copy this pattern onto another sheet of paper in landscape orientation. Use the copy to mark off your progress and keep the original for another project.

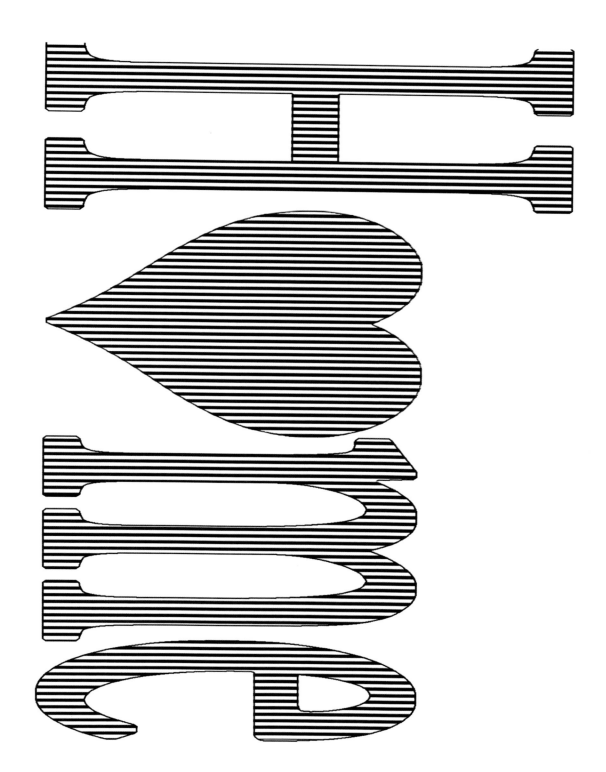

fold back here

uses 418 numbered pages

Pattern 5: Christmas Tree

This pattern uses 306 numbered pages. It looks best when folded with the cut-and-fold method, but it can be folded the conventional way as well (see example on the previous page).

Do not use this original sheet. Copy this pattern onto another sheet of paper in landscape orientation. Use the copy to mark off your progress and keep the original for another project.

Warning: this pattern is a pain to fold using the standard method because of the multiple levels. Do not attempt this pattern as a first exercise unless you use the cut-and-fold method.

fold back here

uses 306 numbered pages

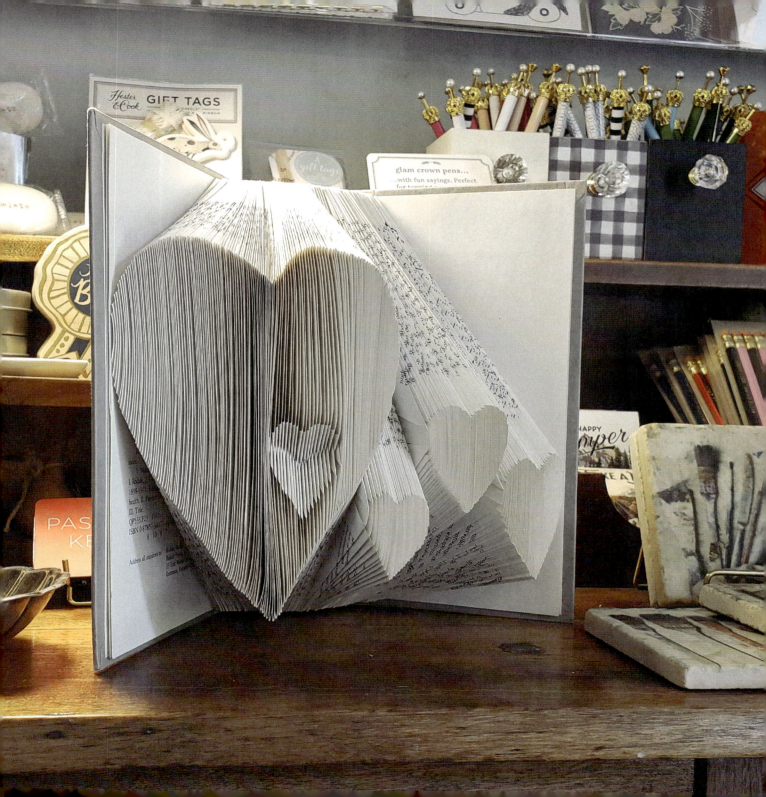

Pattern 6: Mother's Heart

Use 550 numbered pages for this pattern. You can fold this "mother's heart with baby hearts" using the standard method of folding.

Do not use this original sheet. Copy this pattern onto another sheet of paper in landscape orientation. Use the copy to mark off your progress and keep the original for another project.

Optional: use part of this pattern to fold one or more heats without folding the entire pattern. Count both black and white stripes and double that number to determine how many pages you will need for the section you want to use.

Pattern 7: Teapot

Uses 528 numbered pages. Fold this teapot pattern using either the standard method of folding or cut-and-fold.

Do not use this original sheet. Copy this pattern onto another sheet of paper in landscape orientation. Use the copy to mark off your progress and keep the original for another project.

This pattern will be tough to work with because the stripes are so slim. I normally make my patterns fit across the landscape orientation of a printer paper, but this one was made to fit the trim of the book. For best results, scan the image and stretch it out sideways to fit 10 inches on an 8.5 x 11 sheet of paper.

fold back here

uses 528 numbered pages

Pattern 8: Read

This pattern uses 400 numbered pages. It can be folded using either the standard or cut-and-fold methods..

Do not use this original sheet. Copy this pattern onto another sheet of paper in landscape orientation. Use the copy to mark off your progress and keep the original for another project.

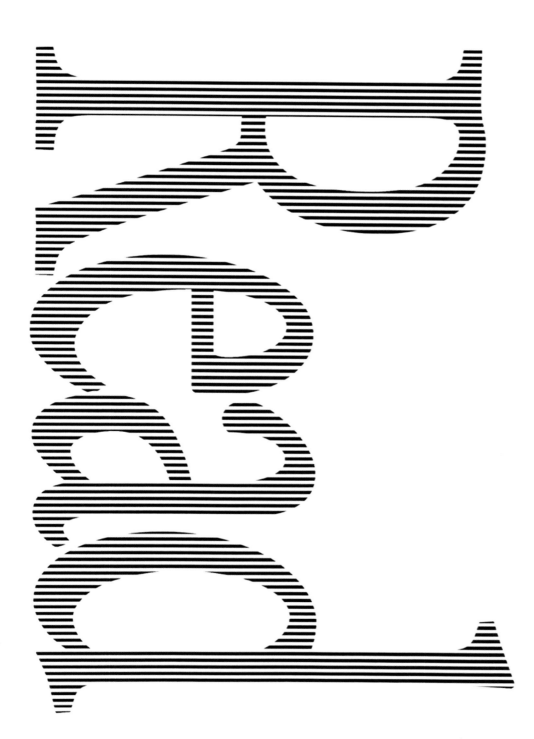

fold back here

uses 400 pages

Pattern 9: US Map Flag

This pattern is a show stopper. It uses 458 numbered pages and is folded using the cut-and-fold method with the first and last tic marks on each page folded back at an angle (see combination fold on page 59).

Prepare your book as instructed for a standard fold book, then mark the entire pattern on the book--every piece of every stripe. Cut all but the first and last markings on each page, then fold each page with the top and bottom at an angle and all other tabs straight back.

Do not use this original sheet. Copy this pattern onto another sheet of paper in landscape orientation. Use the copy to mark off your progress and keep the original for another project.

This pattern is by far the most difficult pattern in this book and can easily fetch $100 at a gift shop.

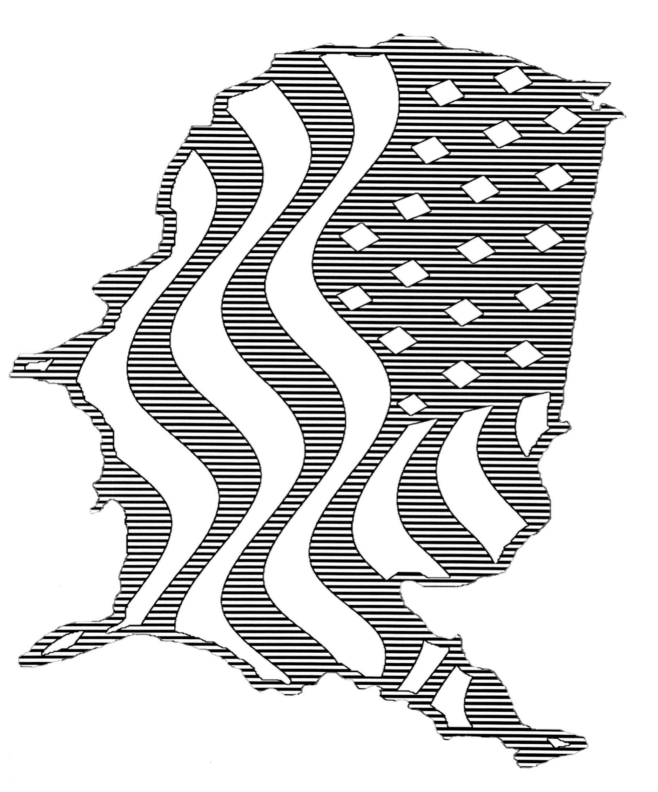

fold back here

uses 458 numbered pages

Pattern 10: Bird House

This pattern uses 350 numbered pages and is folded using a combination of the standard and cut-and-fold methods.

Prepare your book as instructed for a standard fold book, then mark the entire pattern on the book. Fold this book according to the standard method except for the two holes in the center. Cut the markings for the holes only and fold the tabs straight back for the two holes.

Optional: insert and glue a paper straw into the smaller hole and add a paper bird on top of the straw.

Do not use this original sheet. Copy this pattern onto another sheet of paper in landscape orientation. Use the copy to mark off your progress and keep the original for another project.

uses 350 numbered pages

Other Resources

YOUTUBE VIDEOS

My channel DIYMarta on Youtube has several tutorials for book folding that will be helpful to watch before you start. Look for the channel DIYMARTA, and watch tutorials in my Folded Book playlist.

WEBSITE TUTORIALS

You can find more detailed tutorials on my website diymarta.com. Don't be shy about trying out other tutorials on my website like actual book construction or wet felting or even special effects makeup.

FREE STRIPED BACKGROUNDS

On diymarta.com, under the article "Simplified Folded Book Art," there are 5 striped background options: 352 pages, 462 pages, 550 pages, 616 pages, 792 pages. The "pages" refer to numbered pages, not sheets of paper, so take that into consideration when planning your folded book project.

Print your striped background in landscape orientation at about 95% of the original size so all the stripes print around the margins.

Draw your image, fold the top back 1/4 inch to form a tab, and you're ready to work!

ETSY PATTERNS

My Etsy store (etsy.com/diymarta) has several pre-made striped patterns for sale and you can also order a custom-made striped pattern in my shop.

There are a number of other pattern makers on Etsy that use the measure-and-mark method and have tons of ready-made patterns also.

INSTAGRAM @ DIYMARTHA

CUT AND FOLD USING STRIPED PATTERNS

FOLDED BOOK: 1 PATTERN, 3 WAYS

FOLDING BOOKS WITH STRIPED PATTERNS

Made in the USA
Coppell, TX
17 August 2020